YOUR KNOWLEDGE HAS VALUE

- We will publish your bachelor's and master's thesis, essays and papers

- Your own eBook and book - sold worldwide in all relevant shops

- Earn money with each sale

Upload your text at www.GRIN.com and publish for free

Michael A. Braun

Microsoft is a Monopoly, which operates against the Public Interest?!

GRIN Publishing

Bibliographic information published by the German National Library:

The German National Library lists this publication in the National Bibliography; detailed bibliographic data are available on the Internet at http://dnb.dnb.de .

Imprint:

Copyright © 2003 GRIN Verlag GmbH
Print and binding: Books on Demand GmbH, Norderstedt Germany
ISBN: 978-3-656-88079-0

This book at GRIN:

http://www.grin.com/en/e-book/116897/microsoft-is-a-monopoly-which-operates-against-the-public-interest

MICROSOFT IS A MONOPOLY, WHICH OPERATES AGAINST THE PUBLIC INTEREST?!

By Michael A. Braun – EEM/3 (ERASMUS)

You are using a PC? Probably there is a version of Microsoft's Windows operating system running on it. When Microsoft, nowadays with 90% market share the worlds leading operating system producer [Eisenach/Lenard, 2001], years ago started to develop and to distribute Windows the company applied for a worldwide copyright. Which allows them to be the only supplier of this particular software. Therefore Microsoft is a monopoly in the Windows-market and might be one in the whole operating system market. But Microsoft is more than this. They are also producing completing application programs and tools for the Internet. Question is now whether Microsoft is abusing its market power or not. And how this behaviour might affect consumers. This essay is going to outline how their operating system monopoly arose and if this power is transferred into adjacent markets. It will be tried to be both critically and descriptive with a final statement at the end.

First of all it might be helpful to have some definitions as a basic idea. So what means to be a monopoly? According to Waldman/Jensen 'a monopoly is the sole producer of a good for which there are no close substitutes' [2001]. A reason for monopoly might be high barriers of entry [Mankiw, 2001]. This could be (1) a factor of production, which belongs only to this firm. Or (2) a state licence that is only given to this particular company. As well (3) the cost of production could make the difference. Higher volume might make this organization more efficient in terms of economies of scale. And, going on with the question, what might be the public interest in general? On one hand in theory consumers individually want to get most out of their available amount of money, or in other words they want to pay the relative lowest price for the relative highest consume mixes [Mankiw, 2001]. On the other hand they also want to get the highest degree of product quality and rate of product-use. And moreover consumers are as well searching for a high variety of choice in both products and manufacturers. But in terms of a monopoly this might fail. The reason is that there might be only little to no substitutes available.

But how does this theoretical background affect the Microsoft case? Microsoft, as indicated, produces several tools for using computers effectively. According to Eisenach/Lenard it can be assumed that the company has a monopoly and barriers of entry into the operating system market are high [2001]. In general (1) costs for product-development in technology markets are large in the beginning. In terms of software this is also described as large costs of the first copy. But there will be (2) low costs for the replication and distribution of any further copy. And (3) low marginal costs lower average costs. This means the more is produced and sold the lower the relative costs for each single copy are. Furthermore (4) in the software market high switching costs make it difficult for customers to change to another system. An example: In terms of a operation system this might be the price for the new software and the 'sunk costs'[1] for the previous used system. And often the costs of a change are higher than its reached gain. This phenomenon is called 'lock-in' and catches the customers so to say. In this context U.S. management professor Drucker argues 'No new system can displace an established system unless it outperforms it by a factor of ten.' [in: Zerdick/Picot, 1999] . Further on software as a particular good has another interesting characteristic. In this market, so called, net effects (or network externalities) arise. According to Metcalfe's Law this means that the value of a network or system increases with the number of its users in square [in: Zerdick/Picot, 1999]. In other words this are huge demand-side economies of scale. Therefore it can be assumed that this market tends to make entry for new competitors difficult. Summarized it can be said that indeed a singularly product in the beginning of the digital age, huge economies of scale and great network benefits combined with respective switching costs unfolded some kind of sucking effect leading to a natural monopoly for Microsoft. These characteristics mainly helped the company to become the market leader in operating systems rapidly. And the more users the Windows-program had the more completing application programs were written for it.

But in general it is not seen that a firm, which has a monopoly or even a dominant position in one market, is going to leverage[2] this market power into an adjacent market. The risk that all profits might be extracted from the first market would be too high. This is different to Microsoft's situation. Eisenach/Lenard argued that Microsoft had a clear incentive to become dominant in the browser market [2001]. Potential entrants into the operating systems market

---

[1] Investments into the old system: e.g. completing application programs, training of employees and specific hardware.

could step in with the help of their browser software. And once it is installed it can be the basis for a new operating system.

---

[2] So called leveraging-theory. Indicated as being become outdated this theory is not very popular in the US anymore. But the European Commission as reasoning used it while the trusts proceed against Microsoft. Source: Dorfs, J., Abschluss des europäischen Kartellverfahrens vermutlich bis Ende dieses Jahres, Handelsblatt, issue 213, 05.11.2002, p. 18

But if an installed base of application programs that can run only under Windows exists, this creates a massive barrier of entry. Not so Java, Sun's public programming language for applications. This possesses cross-platform compatibility, which allows application programs to be written that could run under nearly every operating system. In that case barriers of entry for competing operating systems are reduced strongly. Therefore to keep company's power over years several actions as are described detailed in the complaint US against Microsoft were taken [Eisenach/Lenard, 2001].

Microsoft's main fear probably was to loose customers of their operating system. If any firm produces a browser - that not necessarily needs Windows as an operating system – this company could have a strong step in the door to Microsoft's core market. According to the judgement of Microsoft's third court process in terms of monopoly between May 1998 and June 2000, the company was accused to have done three main offences [Möschel, 2002]. First they nearly monopolized the operating system market through Windows. Second Microsoft allegedly tried to monopolize the browser market to their favour. Third the company integrated the Microsoft Internet Explorer into the Windows package for free. So there was no need for customers to search for a competing produce. This was described as illegal bundling and competition-hostilely against Netscape, their major competitor in the market for browser software. Additionally it was argued that the company illegally used its dominant Windows operating system to force its way into other markets. In the end of the trail the firm was condemned to decartelise its business into two independent parts, one for operating systems and one for application programs. Problem is that this means a drastically intervention in vested titles of shareholders, one of the principle of free market economy. But Microsoft went into appointment and in June 2001 the responsible Court of Appeals removed the judgement. Instead there was another complaint, that ended in autumn 2002 with relatively mild consequences compared to the previous judgement.

But again, what were the reasons for taking Microsoft to court? What did they do wrong and how is the 'consumer-argument' taken into account? To tackle this question there might by some points, that can be separated into two main strands. Firstly arguments related to every single individual. And secondly the one that are more related to society and the companies competitors. According to Carney/France Microsoft's bundling policy can be seen as the key issue [2001]. This means the company had a practise of continually adding new features to Windows. And because customers were already looked-in to the core product, Microsoft's operating system, it was relatively easy to get customers to use also its additional software. There was no argument for competitors products – even they might have been better. This way of acting could dampen competition and might reduce consumers choice. To go on, this might also reduce technical progress. There might be no longer any reason for competitors to develop new own products and services as long as there is such a dominant firm in the market. On the other side Microsoft itself is searching for new applications. But they are not able to invent that much as could be invented probably by different firms. Therefore the pace of innovation might be slower. And also the variety of applications. Because tools, that allegedly not fit to monopolists portfolio would not be introduced although there might be a demand at the market.

Summarized it can be said that there are some good explanations for Microsoft's monopolistic behaviour. Mainly reasons in leading to more success in business would fit. And probably there is no doubt anymore about Microsoft being a monopoly or not. But it could be much more interesting to have a look whether the company operates against the public interest or not. In this particular market time and fast action are very important. A current monopoly can be worthless soon because products might become obsolete. And reached market positions therefore do not guarantee anything for the future. In this way progress in technology might hinder that Microsoft becomes too lazy. And it also might hinder that the range of products is not too small and consumers do not face dramatically losses of choice. So it can be assumed, Microsoft's monopoly is theoretically against public interest. But this might be in reality not that relevant. Moreover this leads to the question what might be fine at the current situation. First of all the huge net effects are supposed to be good for consumers. If operating systems, completing software etc. would change more often high 'sunk costs' would be generated. Also Microsoft's economies of scale might lead to lower product-prices and better quality in terms of optimisation of products. And caused 'look-in-effects' are a specific characteristic of this particular market which are not illegal or even illegitimate and therefore to be seen as a regular part of competitive behaviour. Also the integration of more and better tools into Windows might be seen as product-improvement which is to the favour of consumers. And it might be taken into account that according to Eisenach/Lenard, if Microsoft has not the monopoly in operating systems probably some other company would have it [2001].

<u>References:</u>

CARNEY, D. and FRANCE, M., 2001. *The Microsoft Case: Tying it all together.* In: Business Week, issue 03.12.2001

EISENACH, J.A. and Lenard, T.M., 2001. *Competition, Innovation and the Microsoft monopoly: Antitrust in the digital marketplace.* 2nd Edition, chapters 1 to 3, Norwell:

LIPCZYNSKI, J., and WILSON, J., 2001. Industrial Organisation – An analysis of competitive markets. Essex: Pearson Education

MANKIW, N.G., 2001. *Grundzüge der Volkswirtschaftslehre.* 2nd Edition, chapters 15 and 21, Stuttgart: Schäfer-Poeschel

MÖSCHEL, W., 2002. *Wettbewerbspolitische Lehren aus einem komplexen Fall – Das Microsoft-Verfahren vor dem Abschluss.* In: NZZ – Neue Züricher Zeitung, issue 10.07.2002

STORBECK, O., 2001. *Microsoft hat sein Monopol missbraucht.* In: Handelsblatt, Nr. 039, issue 23.02.2001

WALDMAN, D.E. and JENSEN, E.J., 2001. *Industrial Organization.* 2nd Edition, chapters 1, 2 and 17, New York:

ZERDICK, A. and Picot, A., 1999. *Die Internet-Ökonomie – Strategien für die digitale Wirtschaft.* Pp. 154 – 178, Berlin:

N.A., 2002. *Abschluss des europäischen Kartellverfahrens vermutlich bis Ende dieses Jahres.* In: Handelsblatt, Nr. 213, issue 05.11.2002

N.A., 2001. *Leaders: A lucky escape; Microsoft.* In: The Economist, issue 10.11.2001